blur
The early years

Wise Publications

London / New York / Sydney / Paris / Copenhagen / Madrid

Bang

Words & Music by Damon Albarn, Graham Coxon, Alex James & Dave Rowntree

1. Sit - ting in an S.___ D. T. wait - ing for an un - der - ground train to
(Verses 2 & 3 see block lyric)

rum - ble un - der - neath___ my feet.

Bang goes an-oth-er day, where it went I could not say,

1. now I'll have to wait an-oth-er week. 2. When

2, 3. do it too. I don't need an-y-one but a

lit-tle love would make things bet-ter. I don't need an-y-one

but a lit-tle love_____ would make things____ bet-ter.

(Instrumental)

Ah

ah_____

ah.

I don't need— a-ny-one_____ but a
lit - tle love_____ would make things_____ bet - ter.

Play 4 times

Verse 2:
When all is said and all is done
What was said was never done
Don't panic it's not really worth your while.
Bang goes another year
In and out of one ear
Everybody is doing it so do it too.

Verse 3:
Sitting on the early bus
Passing through the morning rush
It makes no difference that I'm not with you.
Bang goes another year
In and out of one ear
Everybody is doing it, I'll do it too.

Chemical World

Words & Music by Damon Albarn, Graham Coxon, Alex James & Dave Rowntree

1. The pay - me girl has had e - nough of the bleeps, __ so she
(Verse 2 see block lyric)

takes a bus __ in - to __ the coun - try. Al - though she got her - self

9

Verse 2:
Peeping Thomas has a very nice view
Across the street at the exhibitionist.
These townies they never speak to you,
Just stick together so they never get lonely.
Feeling lead, feeling quite light-headed,
Had to sit down and have some sugary tea.
In a chemical world, in a chemical world
It's very very very cheap.

Colin Zeal

Words & Music by Damon Albarn, Graham Coxon, Alex James & Dave Rowntree

1. Co - lin Zeal knows the va - lue of mass ap - peal, he's a pe - des - tri - an walk - er, he's a
(Verse 2 see block lyric)

ci - vil talk - er, he's an af - fa - ble man with a plau - si - ble plan, keeps his

pleased with him - self,___ ah.___ He's

pleased with him - self,___ he's pleased with him - self,___ he's so

To Coda ⊕

pleased with him - self,___ ah.___ And then he

D.%. al Coda

Verse 2:
While sitting in traffic
Colin thinks in automatic,
He's an immaculate dresser,
He's your common aggressor.
Colin's the modern retard
With a love of bombast,
Keeps his eyes on the news,
Doesn't dwell on the past.

Coping

Words & Music by Damon Albarn, Graham Coxon, Alex James & Dave Rowntree

1. Pri - mal ev - il what am I,
(Verse 2 see block lyric)

tongue tied till the day I die, there's no love made with mer-maids, it's just dis-trac-tion or so they say.

2. It's a

Verse 2:
It's a sorry state you're getting in
The same excuse is wearing thin
There's no self-control left in me
What was not will never will be.

For Tomorrow

Words & Music by Damon Albarn, Graham Coxon, Alex James & Dave Rowntree

and hold-ing on for to-mor-row.

Lon-don ice cracks on a seam-less lie,

he's hang-ing on for dear life,

and so we hold each oth-er tight-ly

21

22

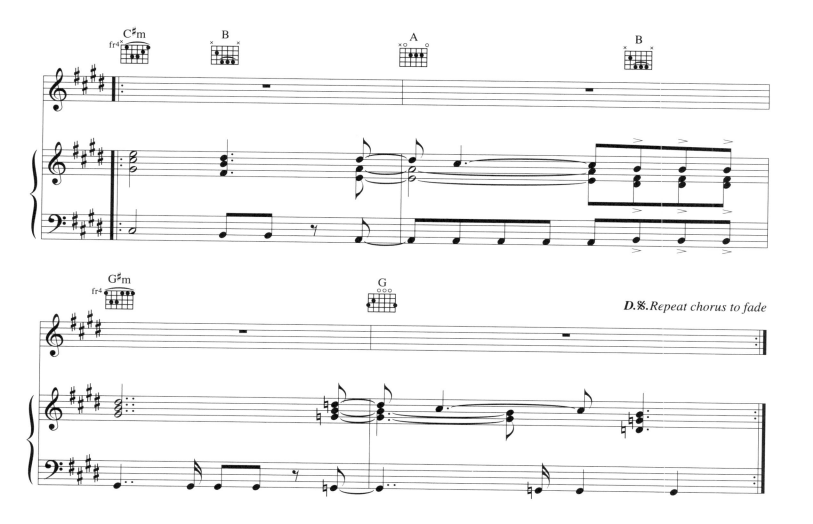

Verse 2:
She's a twentieth century girl
With her hands on the wheel,
Trying not to make him sick again
Seeing what she can borrow.
London's so nice back in your seamless rhymes
But we're lost on the Westway,
So we hold each other tightly
And we can wait until tomorrow, singing…

D.%.
Trying not to be sick again
And hold on for tomorrow.
She's a twentieth century girl
Holding on for dear life,
So we hold each other tightly
And hold on for tomorrow, singing…

Ad lib. spoken over fade
Jim stops and gets out the car
Goes to a house in Emperor's Gate
Through the door and to his room
Then he puts the TV on
Turns it off and makes some tea
Says modern life is rubbish…

Then Susan comes into the room
She's a naughty girl with a lovely smile
Says let's take a drive to Primrose Hill
It's windy there and the view is so nice
London ice can freeze your toes
Like anyone I suppose.

Oily Water

Words & Music by Damon Albarn, Graham Coxon, Alex James & Dave Rowntree

1. Lead in me and me
(Verse 2 see block lyric)
— in wa - ter, dang - ling in my world, — I

swal-lowed too— much oi-ly wa-ter, now it's slip-ping down— my spine.— In a sense of self— in de-cline, grow-ing fat— on sound,— it's on-ly an ear-ly morn--ing dream— and the whole world will be—— al-right.—

Verse 2:
My head hurts with suspicion
I'm coming home sometime
I've swallowed too much oily water
It's slipping down my spine.

A sense of self in decline
I'm lying on my back
It's only an early morning dream
And the whole world will be alright.

Pressure On Julian

Words & Music by Damon Albarn, Graham Coxon, Alex James & Dave Rowntree

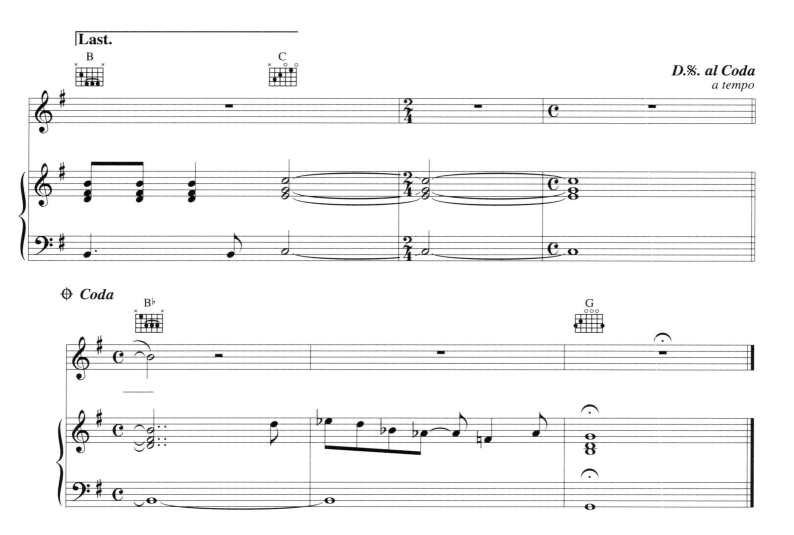

Verse 2:

Swimming in yellow pissy water,
Sand getting in between the ears.
No blood in head in this bloody weather,
Irate people with yellow tongues.
Only the magical transit children
Sing, sing the lullaby, bah bah bah.
Falling into walls, well what is it with you?
You'd never know, never know, never know.

Spoken:

There was pressure on Julian
Pushing trolleys in the car park from B to A,
Then back to B.
Pressure on Julian, he keeps passing out,
Poor, precious little snout.
The birds are singing at night.
Pressure on Julian.

Popscene

Words & Music by Damon Albarn, Graham Coxon, Alex James & Dave Rowntree

Verse 2:
I'm leaving town to run away,
Run into your twisted arms.
No queues and there's no panic there,
Just dangle your feet in the grass.
My lack of natural lustre now
Seems to be losing me friends,
So in the absence of a way of life
I'll repeat this again and again and again.

Slow Down

Words & Music by Damon Albarn, Graham Coxon, Alex James & Dave Rowntree

down. I've al - ways said

it will ne - ver change, all you have to do just be you, I

To Coda ⊕ **1.**

think that's all I want to say.

38

Verse 2:
And all the things I ever told you
I didn't mean at all, I didn't mean at all,
I'd forget you.
So if you come here, if you come here,
All you have to do, just you be you,
I think that's all I want to say to you.

Verse 3:
And all those things that I told you
I didn't mean at all, I didn't mean at all,
I'd forget you.
So if you come here, if you come here,
All you have to do, just you be you,
I think that's all I need to say to you.

She's So High

Words & Music by Damon Albarn, Graham Coxon, Alex James & Dave Rowntree

ev - 'ry____ day_____ I see her____ face_____ it does - n't help____ me.____

She is so____ high, she is so____ high, she is so____ high,

I want to crawl all ov - er her.____ She is so____ high,

she is so____ high, she is so____ high, I want to crawl all ov - er her.____

she does-n't help_____ me._____

Verse 2:
I think of her
Everyday,
I think of her,
It doesn't help me.
I think of her
Everyday,
I think of her,
It doesn't help me.

Sing

Words & Music by Damon Albarn, Graham Coxon, Alex James & Dave Rowntree

Sunday Sunday

Words & Music by Damon Albarn, Graham Coxon, Alex James & Dave Rowntree

dream of pro-tein on a plate,— re-gret you left it quite so late, to

To Coda ⊕

ga-ther the fami-ly round the ta-ble to eat e-nough to sleep.

|1, 2.

(*3º vocal in*)

Oh   the   Sun - day   sleep.

|3.

sleep.

⊕ *Coda*

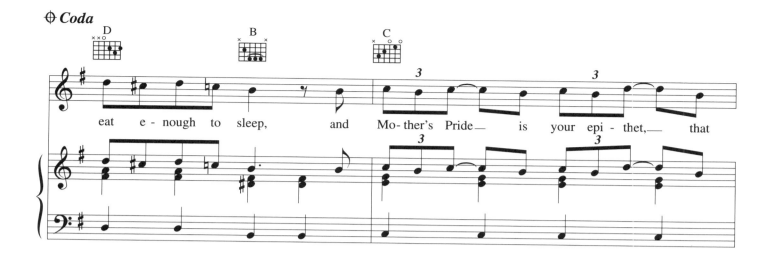

eat e-nough to sleep, and Mo-ther's Pride— is your epi-thet,— that

ex-tra slice you'll soon re-gret, so go-ing out is your best bet, then

rall.

bin-go your-self to sleep. Oh that Sun-day sleep.—

Verse 2:
Sunday Sunday here again, a walk in the park
You meet an old soldier and talk of the past
He fought for us in two world wars
Says the England he knew is no more
He sings the Songs of Praise every week
But always falls asleep.
For that Sunday sleep.

There's No Other Way

Words & Music by Damon Albarn, Graham Coxon, Alex James & Dave Rowntree

Verse 2:
You're taking the fun
Out of everything,
You're making it clear
When I don't want to think.
You're taking me up
When I don't want to go up any more,
I'm just watching it all.

Exclusive Distributors:
Music Sales Limited
8/9 Frith Street, London W1V 5TZ, England.
Music Sales Pty Limited
120 Rothschild Avenue, Rosebery, NSW 2018, Australia.

Order No. AM938190
ISBN 0-7119-5859-9
This book © Copyright 1996 by Wise Publications.
Visit the Internet Music Shop at
http://www.musicsales.co.uk

Compiled by Hilary Donlon.
Music arranged by Roger Day.
Music processed by Paul Ewers Music Design.
Book design by Michael Bell Design.
Photograph supplied by London Features International.

Printed in the United Kingdom by
Caligraving Limited, Brunel Way, Thetford, Norfolk.

Your Guarantee of Quality:
As publishers, we strive to produce every book to
the highest commercial standards.
The music has been freshly engraved and the book has been carefully
designed to minimise awkward page turns and to make playing from it a real pleasure.
Particular care has been given to specifying acid-free, neutral-sized
paper made from pulps which have not been elemental chlorine bleached.
This pulp is from farmed sustainable forests and was produced with special regard for the environment.
Throughout, the printing and binding have been planned to ensure a sturdy,
attractive publication which should give years of enjoyment.
If your copy fails to meet our high standards, please inform us and we will gladly replace it.

Music Sales' complete catalogue describes thousands of titles and is
available in full colour sections by subject, direct from Music Sales Limited.
Please state your areas of interest and send a cheque/postal
order for £1.50 for postage to:
Music Sales Limited, Newmarket Road, Bury St. Edmunds, Suffolk IP33 3YB.